Seek

Maddie

Philip

Apple

# .dog
# joy

Photo Credits: Cover Titan © Shannon Smith; Title page Roxie © Katherine Marie Images; TOC Naboo © Erica Kasper; p. 6 Ann Patchett & Rose © John Dolan; p. 14 Asti © Mieke Vaughn-Arnold; p. 19 Chancy & Joey © Janet Fine; p. 25 Lausche © garrityphoto.com; p. 43 Ava © Mike Miller; p. 48 Phoebe © Kate Carter; p. 51 Maxx & Lucy Blue © Chris Daly; p. 59 Harry Cooper © Stephanie Rausser; p. 70 Sophie © Katherine Murphy; p. 71 Gracie © Jazzi Photos; p. 85 Woody © Shelleye Regan; p. 98 Leo & Claire © Norma Thurman; p. 101 Sugar © Lauren Grabelle; p. 127 Pumpkin © Kristen Hellstrom; p. 132 Sabrina © Lisa Wakida; p. 134 McKenzie © Steve Hessel; p. 147 Gus © Spencer Huang; p. 157 Sophie © Stephanie Squier; p. 160 Baby © Frederick Herrin; p. 169 Comet © Robin Shepett; p. 177 Penny & Nemo © Amanda Jones

Mention of specific companies, organizations, or authorities in this book does not imply endorsement by the author or publisher, nor does mention of specific companies, organizations, or authorities imply that they endorse this book, its author, or the publisher.

Rodale books may be purchased for business or promotional use or for special sales. For information, please write to:
Special Markets Department, Rodale Inc., 733 Third Avenue, New York, NY 10017

Printed in China
Rodale Inc. makes every effort to use acid-free ♾, recycled paper ♻.

Book design by Cameron Woo and Steve Barretto

**Library of Congress Cataloging-in-Publication Data**

Dogjoy : the happiest dogs in the universe / by the editors of The Bark.
     p.   cm.
   ISBN-13 978–1–60529–730–9 hardcover
   ISBN-10 1–60529–730–5 hardcover
   1. Photography of dogs.   2. Dogs—Pictorial works.   3. Dogs--Humor.   I. Bark (Berkeley, Calif.)   II. Title: Dog joy.
TR729.D6D6485  2009
779'.329772—dc22                      2009022967

Distributed to the trade by Macmillan

2  4  6  8  10  9  7  5  3  1  hardcover

**We inspire and enable people to improve their lives and the world around them**

For more of our products visit **rodalestore.com** or call 800-848-4735

# .dog joy

## The Happiest Dogs in the Universe

By the Editors of *The Bark*

Roxie

# Smiling
## DOGS

Naboo

# FOREWORD

nce I sit down on the couch with my computer to write this, once I get really comfortable with all the pillows in the right place, my dog Rose approaches and, panting on the last warm night before I break down and turn on the air conditioning, smiles at me. Rose is a white Terrier-Chihuahua sort of dog who is pushing 14. It's been two or three years since she's been able to jump up on the couch by herself, and she never decides that she wants to be up here with me until I am in exactly the right position.

But now that I am and now that she does, I put the computer on the floor and get up to lift her to the spot she likes by my knees. She drops her muzzle over my shin and sighs heavily in a way I take to be a combination of gratitude and contentment, although it's possible that it is simply a sigh of entitlement. We are both very happy this way or, I should say, I am happy. My assumption of Rose's happiness is based on the smile and then the sigh, the languid licking on my calf that's her way of winding down before sleep—all the things I've come to count as communication from her to me.

There are, of course, plenty of people who will tell you that the expression on a dog's face that is open of mouth and squinty of eye is not a smile in the same sense as a human smile, and that when a dog licks your calf, it is not love but an instinctual desire for food or a grooming ritual because you are a member of her pack and that is her job.

Okay then, let's not burden these dogs with our human projections. Look through these photographs and do not assume that just because that mouth is in very much the same position your mouth was in when you got the bicycle you desperately wanted for your ninth birthday or heard a very funny dirty joke after two glasses of champagne that we can call it a smile. In short, do not speak for these dogs, do not assume their joy, just have some joy of your own. Look at them squirming and rolling and leaping and laughing and let them do what dogs do best: give us an effervescent dose of wordless euphoria.

My dog Rose is looking at me now, her head on my leg. It's hard not to assume that she is deeply in love with me, because the only times in my life I've looked at someone that way there was a great deal of love involved. I guess the only thing I can be sure of and therefore have the right to speak to, is that I am deeply in love with her. That's enough.

Sometimes, the best moments in human relationships are the ones in which we have the self-restraint to say nothing at all, to demonstrate our love and joy instead of trying to break down the experience and reshape it into words. This is the genius of dogs, one of the many geniuses of dogs—they have the nonverbal-expression thing down cold. And if we're reading too much into everything they're not saying, then so be it. They'll forgive us. They always do.

—Ann Patchett

Peppy

# INTRODUCTION

A few years ago, a reader sent us a snapshot of her smiling dog, Peppy, and suggested that we include it in our magazine, *The Bark*, and launch a Smiling Dog contest. We thought it was a great idea, and did just that. Since then, we've published thousands of photos—both in the magazine and online—of dogs displaying their boundless enthusiasm for life. Each time I open my e-mail, I'm greeted by a batch of new entries—I ooh and aah over the sweetest of puppies, romp with the pack, take adventure-filled trips or am moved by the sincere seniors. I feel that I must have the best job in the world. Not only do I get to befriend these joyous dogs, but I'm also able to introduce them to the readers of my magazine and now to you, the readers of this book.

Smiling, the purest form of communication, is indeed universal—we do it, dogs do it. Want proof? You'll find it here. Dig in, delight awaits . . . here come the smiling dogs!

—Claudia Kawczynska
Editor-in-chief, *The Bark*

# YOU'RE HOME

---

Only gone for a day. A few hours.
For a quart of milk. And there
they are, their bright, tongue-waggy
faces at the window, at the door
as it opens, their furry feet pawing
at our pant legs in happy reunion.
Luggage dropped. Laptop laid down.
Milk set on counter. We're on the
ground, they're in our arms.
We're theirs. They're ours.
We're home.

**FRANKIE** stands proud on his porch. He smiles into the sun and watches the white cat across the street.

**Sammy**

Sammy loved to hunt for lizards, which were abundant in our backyard on Iberville Street in New Orleans, where we lived before Hurricane Katrina. But he didn't have much luck catching them. So on this day when his daddy arrived home from work with a lizard for him, Sammy was beside himself with joy.

**SOPHIE**
is an exuberant
little dog with a
passion for life,
biscuits and walks
in the woods.

Both dogs are Save a Sato rescues from Puerto Rico and now serve as the welcoming committee, greeting visitors to our home with their smiles.

BENJI
loves to run
full speed
to greet me.

Asti

Quinn

Molly

DogJoy is running
toward your human.
PeopleJoy is knowing
your dog is smiling
because she's running
toward you!

Jesse

**Belle** is a homeless dog at an all-breed rescue who enthusiastically greets all who come in, positive that they are there only to take her home!

Cooper is equal parts sweet and sassy. Seen here enjoying his job as a backyard wood chipper.

Fern

"WHAT TOOK YOU SO LONG?"

Cory & Shelby

Juliette & Petey

Welcome

Simon

Squid

Waggin'

Edgar

Chancy
& Joey

Mimi is always the first one at the door to greet us with a BARK!

BARK! BARK!

# SWEETIES

———

Hail the sweeties, the pups
who melt into a puddle at your feet
with the first touch or scratch.
The ones who offer those soft,
warm nuzzles that invariably
bring on the giggles, the ones who
magically spark any moment with
a smile that says, without a doubt,
"Guess what? I love you!"

BLUE's photo was taken on his first day in his forever home. It captures the joy and innocence of this newly weaned rescue pup and reaffirms that life is good, people can be kind and strangers can make a difference.

Piper

Piper loves to cuddle in laps (the kids call her a "lapsnatcher"), toss her dog food into the air and catch it, play tug-o-war, and chase sandpipers at the beach.

Addie Mae

Henry

Cooper

Duke

Bella

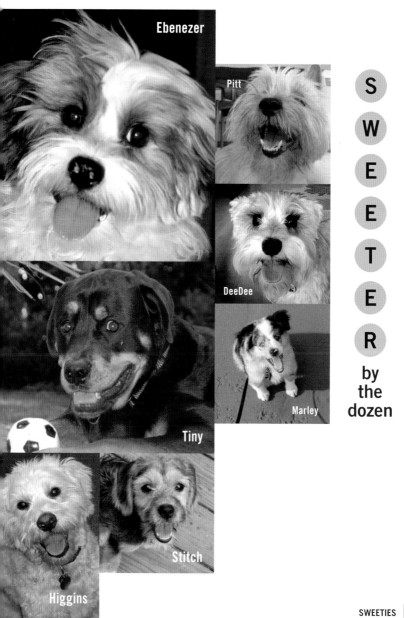

Ebenezer

Pitt

DeeDee

Marley

Tiny

Higgins

Stitch

# SWEETER by the dozen

Rascal was lying on Mom's side, basking in the sun as we cruised around the lake in our pontoon boat.

Rascal

Maeby

As a baby, Maeby had the habit of falling quickly asleep the moment she stepped on grass, almost as if she had been hypnotized. I took this picture on the first day she realized the green stuff wasn't just for snoring—it was also the place we threw a blue squishy thing called a ball. She was simply delighted.

Mercury

Look at those eyes: dark little pools of pure sweetness. When he's not sleeping on your feet, surfing the counters for a snack or herding squirrels, Mercury is smiling with those eyes . . . .

**FINNEGAN**
Rolling in the grass, belly rubs, a warm lap and treats all make me smile.

Charlie's first haircut— Don't I look great?

Simon climbing high up on kitty's tower.

CHUCK's favorite things are fetch, sticks, toilet paper, brushing and singing.

Emma

Zsa Zsa

Lily

Leonardo

Judy

Sumo

Through her eyes and ears, she tells me so many things. Here, it's simply "Can I please have my treat already?"

Muffin

# LAUGHERS

---

The noble hound of historic
paintings, on a hill, proud and
stalwart...forget all that.
We applaud the clowns of the
canine world, those dogs who look
like they get the punch line, even if
the joke is a shredded-up shoe or
the extra treat they just snuck.
They're in love with life's
uproariousness, and we're in
love with them.

**SOPHIE**
loves to laugh, especially after a day of chasing her rubber pig.

CIRCE's joyous grin reveals gratitude and anticipation of a good night's sleep after climbing a 14,000-foot peak.

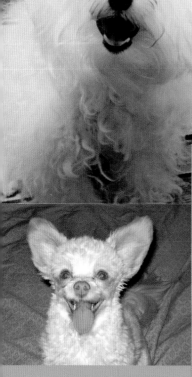

**Monkey** tries on different looks and finally settles on a dazzling, eye-catching grin and perhaps hamming it up a bit.

**Tuffy** loves playing fetch and jumping on my bed to bring me the toy.

## TIGER

What makes
Tiger smile?
Peanut butter.
Cream cheese.
A fresh marrow
bone. Jumping
through hoops
or onto my lap.
Chasing anything
that runs fast.
But most of all,
being with me.

**PUMPKIN**

"When I smile, people always smile back."

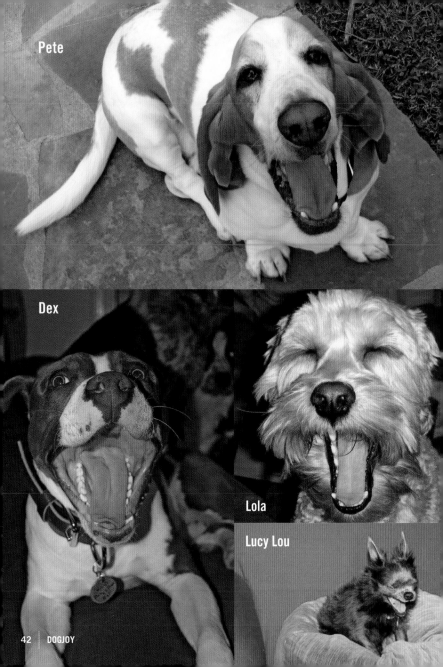

Pete

Dex

Lola

Lucy Lou

Ava

Cocoa

Cooper

Houston

Bobby

Abbey is always happy to help around the kitchen—so long as she doesn't end up on the dinner table!

**SCOOTS**
loves going for car rides, chuckling with delight in the backseat.

**GUINNESS**
A natural comic, loves laughing at his own jokes.

# ADVENTURERS

Dogs are our intrepid co-pilots and fellow adventurers. Nothing makes them smile more than sniffing out new territory or simply covering a worn path with us. Convivial, curious, generous with discoveries and oh so brave—what more can be asked of a traveling companion? They're our perfect partners in fun.

**ARRINGTON**
is happiest when
adventures rule
the day.

BEAR'S FIRST HIKE WITHOUT A LEASH, SO SHE WAS FREE TO ENJOY THE BEAUTIFUL DAY—
THE FLOWERS TASTED SO DELICIOUS.

**PHOEBE**
takes in the
360-degree
view after a
three-hour hike.

HAVOC
helps us
blaze new
trails.

**REILLY** takes a breather during a chaparral exploration.

Maxx and Lucy Blue hiking around Utah's Arches National Park; in the background is the Corona Arch. The dogs were visiting from Colorado and pretty

happy to be in the desert warmth, but after a few days, they were glad to get their paws off slickrock and back in snow!

MAX
especially loved
climbing up
boulders and
feeling the wind
blow through
his ears!

**RUBY**
loves hiking
and discovering
mud puddles.

Liberty & Madison

Austin

Roxy

Dog-tired
is the most
delicious kind
of tired.

Ninja

Tuckerman

Katie

Sadie

Santorini

Ming

Gordon & Pepper

Missy
&
Oscar

Buster

Sophia & Charlotte     Sherman     Boo     Socrates     Clara & Quazzi

THE SMELL OF LEAVES AND WILDFLOWERS: GOOD. THE FEEL OF FRESH AIR ON MY TONGUE: BETTER.
THE TASTE OF FRESH HORSE POOP: BEST.

Daisy & Tulip     Pepsi     Gaby     Ollie     Magnys & Oswald

Oscar

# JOKERS

We have many names for our joker dogs: Ham, Goofball, Comedian, Silly Girl. What they have in common is a love of mischief, humor and fun. These modern-day court jesters are the first to steal our slippers, hide the chew-toy and laugh at even our lamest jokes. They tolerate the silly songs we make up about them, and sometimes they even sing along. These dogs are proof that laughter is indeed the best medicine.

Harry Cooper

Two dogs are chatting during a break at obedience school. One says, "Yeah,

Freedom & Glory

it's a great class, but I don't feel like I'm learning anything I'm going to use in the real world."

Nikko & Cookie

DID YOU HEAR THE ONE ABOUT THE CAT WHO WALKED INTO A BAR?

Charley & Bella

Frank

# Smile—You're on Canine Camera!

Emmit

Cheyenne

Tuesday

He's best friends with a neighbor's pet bunny, he adores
tuna fish, and he likes nothing better than to be chased
around the house with a broom!

OTTO sits in the baby pool after a long day of playing with the kids.

April and Jack
were playing a game of hide-and-seek
in the backyard, while keeping a flock of
hens and the cat amused.

Happy and Opie,
best friends and neighbors, share
a private joke.

# SINCERE

Sincerity is a virtue, it's said,
and is anything more sincere than
a canine smile? Reflections of dogs'
honest hearts and capacity for joy,
these smiles remind us that reveling
in the moment and sharing that
pleasure with our companions are
surefire ways to happiness.

In 2002 we adopted this little guy from a woman who had 80 rescued dogs on the outskirts of Dallas. We named him Mr. Tuvok after the lieutenant commander from *Star Trek Voyager*, since he was to become our security officer. He had a big heart, bum leg and bad teeth, but we fixed him up. And he took good care of our hearts after that.

Mr. Tuvok

Sophie

Gracie loves having her photo taken. If you have a camera,

she won't leave you alone until you take her pic.

Sophie works her charm on potential masseurs and treat donors. She has a keen eye (and nose) for cargo-shorts pockets and is not too proud to beg.

Jake has pretty much been smiling since the day I adopted him.

Sincerity is the

Millie

Molson

Max

Sophie

Logan

Lucy

Rowdy

dog's gift to us.

Fenway

Elmo

Jasmine

Arnie

Pete

Daisy Doo

Cookie

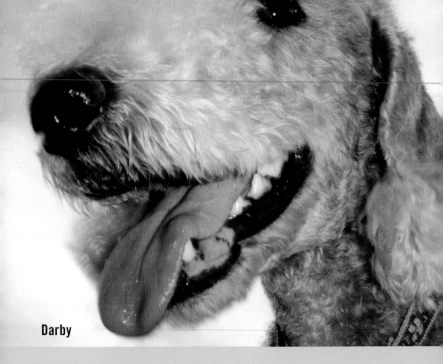

**Darby**

Born to make us laugh and smile, Ms. Darby moves the skies and the heavens above to get our attention to tell us her latest jokes.

Yoshi

Yoshi gets sincere pleasure at the smiles she receives from everyone she meets. She lights up the room when she appears.

My old dog has never seen a throne,
He has never seen a King or Queen.
I think he would be happier with a bone,
Than with any Royal I have ever seen.

— *My Old Dog*, Bernard Shaw

**Nellie**

**Blues**

It doesn't take much to make this senior Nellie smile.

With her constant anticipation of pure joy, Blues, 11, is often mistaken for a pup half her age.

**Mimi**

**Glory**

Mimi's 12th birthday
was celebrated eating
doggie cake for photos.

Joy is finding your
forever family, even if
it's at 10 years old!

He's the happiest boy in the world, charming, devoted, absolutely brilliant, exuberant. . . he's actually a little boy trapped in a doggie body (sort of like Pinocchio).

Yoda

# GRINNERS

------

A grin is the apotheosis
of a smile, and dogs know just
when to flash one. Whether it's a
quick show of pearly whites or a
huge, ear-to-ear display like
the proverbial Cheshire subset,
the memory of a dog's grin lingers
long after her tail stops wagging.
Their joyfulness is impossible
to resist.

ANGUS is a character and a clown.
He keeps us laughing daily with his comical antics.

# Grin and the whole pack grins with you.

**Arthur**

**Neumacks**

He is very mischievous and he laughs each time he gets into trouble!

Neumacks charms us with his elfin grin.

**Piper**

**Rosie**

"Oh happy
   day. . . . Going
   for a ride!!"

"I can't help it;
when you tickle
my head like that,
    I just want
       to grin."

## Chloe

Chloe was smiling because she wanted the steak dinner her family was eating.

Lily

## Sophie

Sophie shares her love of singing. A little hidey-ho from me and the howling begins.

**Mr. Bogart**

"I know nothing of the ransacked bathroom waste-basket and the chewed-up tissues and cotton balls."

**Curly**

**Maddie**

**Woody's** Uncle Buck was a smiling dog and passed down the talent.

# Basking
## in the
## pleasures
## of a
## dog's life.

Shadow

# FIRST FRIENDS

---

When dogs find their soul mates, kindred spirits, matches for their hearts, they just want to spend every minute rolling/running/pawing/playing together. That the kindred spirits are smaller and sillier and sweeter than the big people is a plus. That they'll get down on the ground and giggle is a double plus.

**REBECCA & TONALA**
Happy to be with
my very best pal
(and the feeling
is mutual).

### Kayla & Chewie

Chewie is excited when Kayla returns home from school.

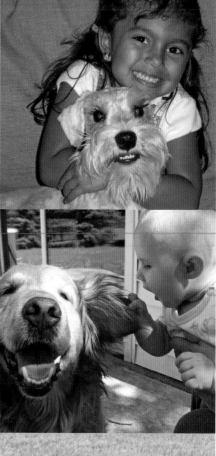

### Buddy & Owen

Buddy has been a great source of entertainment for five-month-old Owen, who lights up whenever he sees him. If I say, "Where's the doggie?" Owen will look down to see where he is.

### Pierson & Max

Max welcomes a "back rub" from his favorite girl.

**Twister & Chloe**

We celebrated the arrival of our adopted niece, Chloe, from China. The photo was taken on Chloe's first visit to my house. Twister usually wears a very somber expression, but that day, he must have felt the joy as Chloe made us all smile.

## Jay & Alex

Coaxing a smile out of Jay, a one-year-old Shar-Pei, requires the skill of his boy, Alex, and the "you hit the spot" spine-tingling belly rub technique.

## Maddy, Reggie & Jillian

Hugs and many licks.

## Chino & Dori

A long walk on a summer day followed by a big hug from Chino's favorite girl.

Murphy & Marley

Murphy's favorite place is in the middle of the couch, even better when shared with his little pal, Marley.

My niece, Allie, insisted we purchase
party hats and a treat for Lupi's birthday.

### Patrick & Portia

Portia is a rescued racing Greyhound. A major reason for her joy is the love of her boy, Patrick.

### Jessie & Brodie

Pure heart and soul smiles make every day worthwhile.

### Nina, Violet & Melissa

Helping homeless dogs can be fun—good exercise, too, for these two young volunteers.

## Kasper & Kat

Why is it so wonderful for a child to have a pet? It is the joy in her eyes, the love in her heart and the compassion for all living things.

## Wally & Meaghan

Wally just loves kids! He's happiest lounging around with his best buddy, Meaghan. At 150 pounds, he has plenty of tummy to rub and plenty of love to share.

# Celebrating
## Midsommar in Dalarana, Sweden.

**Sandra & Nimbus**

Elizabeth & Birdie

Leo & Claire

Travis, Veda & Jasmine

Nyssa & Ali

True Love

Jacoby & Keely

Margaree & Duncan

Eloise & Lammy

Isaiah, Moshe & Sasha

Hannah & Sparky

Honey & Maddie

# SNICKLERS, WINKLERS & GOOGLERS

Where's a mirror? These dogs—with their one-of-a-kind grins and winks and furrowed brows and crooked smiles—just have to see what they look like. Oh, forget the mirror, we'll tell them: Pups, your oh-so-individual expressions are very you, very special and very euphoria-producing.

Sugar

Back from scattering birds, all dogs **SWAGGER** a bit.

Ceasar loves hummus, eats it with celery, carrots or "on" the fingers too.

Ceasar

"Mom is always taking my picture and it drives me nuts. She took this one of me trying to escape being dumped in the pool at the annual Dog Paddle event."

Mochaccino

Barkley

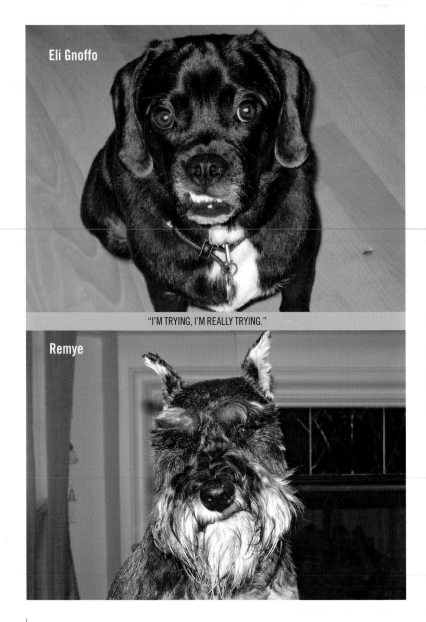

Eli Gnoffo

"I'M TRYING, I'M REALLY TRYING."

Remye

**CHICKORY** was very excited to open her first present! She had lots of fun shredding the wrapping paper to get to her new toy.

Buster

Adie

Uno

Walter

Carmelo

Dublin

Bogart

Pinto Bean

Abbie

Ruby

# Lap time? Is it lap time?

Wendy

NOT SURE I HEARD WHAT YOU SAID. · · · · · · · · · · · · · · · · · · · · · ·

Sophie

Scout

Old Blue Eye is back.      Catching the sunlight.

Hank

Lola

Zella & Willie

Snowy dog Willie
eyes little Zella,
new on the scene;
young dogs cause
trouble, you know.

Taz was so excited because every time the flash went off, he got a treat.

# WATERDOGS

---

Splash! A certain coterie of
tail-waggers happily trades terra
firma for floating blissfully
in the nearest pool or lake.
It's called "dog paddling" for a
reason—dogs invented it, and
when you think up something
famous, you tend to beam
about it. Boastful?
Sure, but who wouldn't be?

**PETEY**
Even this
pint-sized
paddler loves
to swim!

Bella

Waddling and playing in the pond was a favorite pastime.

Mollie, Mandy, Tucker & Tilly

summer pool party anyone?

Chimi

Julia

Albert Edward

Sydney

A bath, a rinse, a dip: **ahhhh**

## Lida Mae

NO swimmer she—
think water buffalo.
But wading in the
shallows at the dog
beach while fetching
a rubber duck filled
her with palpable joy.

## Hunter, Remy & Nera Sue

All they ever wanted to do
was to chase balls and then jump
into the kiddie pool.

## Lexi

What makes Lexi
(and most dogs)
happiest are the
simple things in life:
a treat, a walk to the
park, a back scratch
and getting in the car
to go to the beach.

## Grace

A day on the lake
with the sun on her back
and wind in her fur.

## Ella

Country gal Ella smiles even more when she shares her stream with foster dogs from our local humane society.

## Hunter & Autumn

A treat held high helped my wet dogs—fresh from their lake swim—hold still for the photo.

## Daisy

At the beach, a lake, a river or even a puddle deep enough to lay down in, Daisy, a Nova Scotia Duck Tolling Retriever, is a true waterdog.

# HOW DO I LOOK?

Bunny ears for the Easter parade, reindeer antlers for the annual Christmas card, a tiny blue yarmulke for the neighbor dog's bark-mitzvah, a garland of marigolds in honor of the Hindu bride and groom. What our dogs won't do for a few laughs and a peanut-butter biscuit! And a doggie birthday party? Go ahead, eat the cake—the whole thing! Straight off the floor! And all we have to do is wear a cone-shaped hat? Sign us up!

Som

"I wag, skip, doze, drool over food, dribble over shoes and lark around with my pals. And I SMILE now that I have a home. I even smile at the cats when they let me share their food." (Som was rescued from the streets of Bangkok and is a perfect spokesdog for SCAD, Soi [street] Cats and Dogs in Thailand.)

Boomer

Lola & Leia

Friday, Rambo & Maevis

Kasper

## Party Dogs! Did I hear someone say cake?

Winnie

Medford

Dixie

Kermit

Klowee

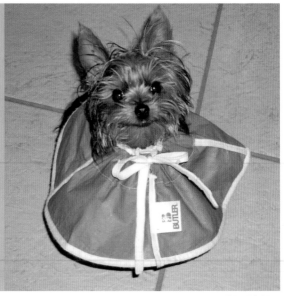

Peanut
(at only three pounds)
makes do with the
smallest post-op
kitty cone.

Easton
"I'm the happy birthday boy!"

Sienna & Zuki

**Beatrix & Cleo**

Sunflower Girls!

**Max**

Pure delight hosting 50 other Bichons!

**Gideon**

Caught taking a cat nap.

**Pumpkin**

Cheers to Pumpkin— she's sweet 15!

**Tasha**

"If I could just stick my nose a little farther under this mossy fence. What? Moss on my face?"

**Sugar**

Prettied up and raring to go.

Wrinkles should merely indicate were smiles have been.
—Mark Twain

Headra

Georgia's
message to us all—
Bee Happy!

# EARNEST

---

Dogs understand the importance
of being earnest—it's built into
their genetic code. Our most devoted
companions display their loyalty
and constancy with unbridled
enthusiasm and grace. Of the many
lessons dogs impart to us, one
of the most important is that being
earnest is at the heart of the
finest relationships.

Lexie

SABRINA
First time experiencing stimulating smells and sounds of the ocean— I feel like a puppy again.

GRACIE is a deaf dog, rescued from a puppy mill and happy as can be.

COWBOY
A source of constant delight.

STORM is a rescue dog, successful at agility and responsive to commands in both English and American Sign Language.

All knowledge—
the totality of all questions
and answers—is contained
in the dog.

—Franz Kafka

**McKenzie**  **Soda**  Ike

Atlas                    Gabriel                    Lily

Esther

Shadow

Oscar

Gus

Shadow

Elvis

PEARL is an enthusiastic lover of life and has had an amazing 15 years. We are grateful for her spirit and longevity.

Their heads are hung with ears
that sweep away the morning dew...

—Shakespeare

Morgan

Koko

Papaya

Riley

Brendan

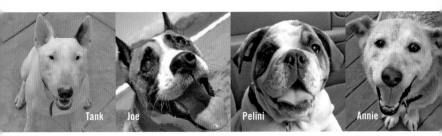

## My favorite things:

bones, daily walks, bones,
pillows, naps, bones, dinner,
rides, bones

Beau

# "A" for EFFORT

One corner of the mouth up.
Then the other. C'mon, corner—
go up. You can do it, you can do it!
Now, wag just the very tippity
end of your tail. Wait, where's
everybody going? Oh, they're
coming back with cameras. Well,
of course—you're adorable!

**DARCY**
Whether it is a walk,
a treat or a cuddle,
Darcy knows how to
get what she wants.

Seven-week-old Zachary taking a rest and feeling quite proud of himself! He had just climbed a few big steps in his new backyard.

# Future Smilers in Training!

Magnuson

Zachary

Sonny

Horus

Mugsy

Violet

Hank

Jude

The
reward
is in
the
effort.

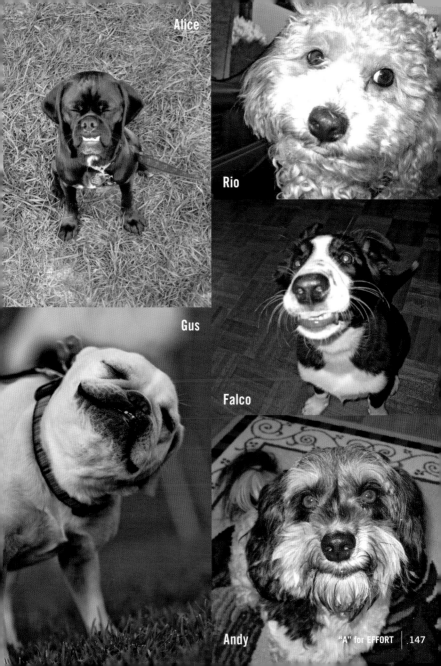

Alice

Rio

Gus

Falco

Andy

Lulu

Zoe's best impersonation of an old person smiling toothlessly.

"I like birthdays (it's always mine, every day), blue balls, blue pools, liver-on-a-stick and, of course, my forays to Poodle World."

Smokey smiles every time he hears his humans' voices.

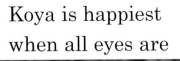

Koya is happiest
when all eyes are
on her—hard to
resist this smile.

Paula sat in the cool grass under her
favorite tree and found joy in the breeze, · · ·
the birdsong and the moment.

Sadie

Sadie, a therapy dog in training, enjoys chasing lizards,
watching horses and curling up in our laps.

Paula

**Spencer** turned 11 weeks old the day this photo was taken. He had been romping in the woods with his brother on a fresh layer of snow: **puppy bliss!**

# AT PLAY

---

There are the reach-for-the-sky
leaps, the tug-tug-tugs with a
holey sock, the squirm-on-the-back
moments, the you-can't-catch-me
dashes around the yard.
But no matter what the playtime
inclination, the "this-is-a-blast"
ear-to-ear beaming is a
happy constant.

**SCOTCH**

This leaper knows no bounds.

This was really the first time that Marley discovered how fast his little legs could go— he ran and ran for hours!

**Sophie**

Unabashed joyous
beach fun.

**Scout**

Often we go to
the park with one
ball and come
home with three
or four. He has
quite a nose for
finding lost balls.

"I don't play accurately—
anyone can play accurately—but I play
with wonderful expression."

—Oscar Wilde

Boudreaux

Patrick

Twinkie

Baby

Baby, our English Mastiff, is playing her favorite game of "chase my best friend, Chopper the Rottie, through the woods." She never catches him but loves the game.

**Sam & Dazy**

Horsing
around
on Mom's
bed.

**Ivy**

"A really
muddy stream
with ducks?
Yes, life just
doesn't get
ANY better."

**Jessie**

Cavorting
at Chicago's
Montrose
Dog Beach.

**Maggie &
Mulligan**
Practice
lessons.

**Chip**
Wwwwweeee!!
Here I come.

**Peanut**
Joy in his
heart while
running
free at the
dog park.

BAILEY & EMMA
Dog vacation to the vast, sandy beaches of the Oregon Coast. Pure bliss!

**YOGI**
Absolute glee for both Yogi and all those who watch him joyously running.

# PERKY

---

Full of life, ready to have fun
(or cause trouble) at a moment's
notice, our perky friends are
Odes to Joy all by themselves.
The simplest occurrence sends these
dogs into spasms of ecstasy.
*She's picking up her car keys.*
*Hallelujah, a ride! And what's that,*
*the leash? A walk!* These canine
dancers, prancers and vixens
announce the good news of the
day with joyous barks.

MUNCHIE loves going to the dog park to play with his friends. Every time we go, his little face lights up with joy.

Celeste    Jackson

Boomer    Simon    Teemu    Sandy

Slick    Kaffee    Conor

# Joie de Canine

Comet

**GINGER** was one of the dogs rescued from Michael Vick's Bad Newz Kennels in April 2007. She was sent to the SPCA for Monterey County a few months later—she was extremely timid and fearful. She became my foster dog and for many months cowered in the kennel and would not accept any kind of affection. **GINGER** has now come out of her shell and finally understands that "This is my life!" and is the happy dog she deserves to be.

Django

Isabelle

Diggity

Daisy

Astro

Jake

Reason

Buttercup

Roxy

Abe

Giddy

Joey

Sebastian

Kai

Daisy

Dharma

Skipper is a huge flirt and knows just what to do to wrap you around his little paw. He smiles and dances for anyone whose attention he wants.

Skipper

Casper

# PACK

Spend time with a pack of
happy dogs and you are reminded
that life is supposed to be fun.
How about a game of six-way
tug-a-rope? Or a splashing swim
across the pond, racing to be
the first to retrieve the stick?
Our dog packs love to love, to laugh,
to play, to steal each other's treats
and toys, to chase and be chased,
and—best of all—to mound up
together for a group snuggle and
a well-earned snooze.

## PENNY & NEMO

Smiling through a rough start: Penny was found malnourished, lying in a ditch with a broken pelvis and a will to survive. She secured a loving home with Nemo, Penny's "mini me" Beagle companion, who was born with a deformed leg—together this Texas duo found the sweet life.

Daisy, Katie, Annabelle & Danielle

Daisy, Dudley & Chester

Abby, Kooper, Lucy, Kiah, Chester, Bailey, Joliet, Taz & Andy

Oreo, Ricky & Ethel

Duke & Romeo (bench)
Docena, Novak, Rodrigo & Wayne

Greta & Audrey

Titus, Sadie & Hunter

Lily, Maggie & Blues

Destiny, Maggie, Taz,
Savannah & Misty

# Dogfriends, doglaughs, dogsmiles, dogfun, doglove

Jig, Trace, Jammer, Mick, Ukiah, Dharma & Spencer

**Boomer, Sam & Gracie Lou**

These three love sitting together, even posing for a photo.

Raya & Jeter

**Our dogs smile when we sing to them — while clapping our hands, of course!**

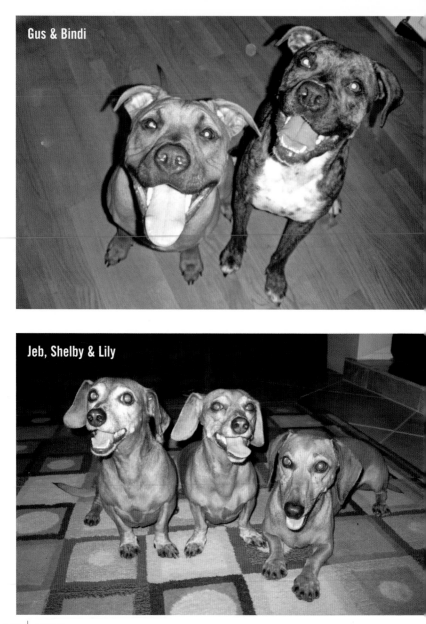

Gus & Bindi

Jeb, Shelby & Lily

Stella, Rudy & Scout

Oso, Molly & Toby

Fatney & Shelly

# Forever Friends!

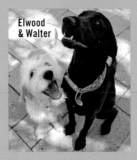

Elwood & Walter

Dixie & Abby

Daffny  Bennett  Blue  Bagel  Denali  Woody  Jagger  Fernie

## ACKNOWLEDGMENTS

We'd like to thank, first and foremost, all the *Bark* readers who sent us photographs of their smiling dogs. For the past eight years, I have been on the receiving end of these e-mails—they help me start the day with a smile and give me a boost throughout the day.

One of our most challenging tasks was to select the 500 smilers needed for this book from the tens of thousands of your photos. Though all dogs do smile in one way or another, some have an uncanny talent for it, and those are the ones whose faces you see here. Dogs also express their joy in other ways—a wag of a tail, a sprightly bounce, a happy howl—and we toast them, too.

We would also like to acknowledge the everyday heroes working in shelters across the country, whose tireless dedication brings joy to the animals in their care. We're especially grateful to the shelters who have sent us smiling dog photos so that we can publish their hopeful faces in every issue of *Bark*. This added cachet has prompted more than a few successful adoptions! In fact, Belle (page 15) was one of the lucky ones; after a very long wait, she recently found her forever home.

We'd like to thank some of our favorite writers—Lee Harrington, Laurie Notaro and Alysia Gray Painter—who contributed their charming, humorous and on-point prose to enrich the beginning of each chapter. Lee's work can be found on pages 58, 120, 166 and 176. Laurie contributed the "Sweeties" intro on page 22, and Alysia's writing graces pages 10, 36, 88, 100, 112, 142 and 154. We have "verbal cartoonist" Dan Liebert to thank for the inspiring *DogJoy* title and for his "brevities" on pages 54 and 101. A nod to Marc Spitz for his insightful joke found on page 60. To our literary agent, Lisa Bankoff, we offer a play bow for her enthusiasm and support. In our next life, we would like to come back as Ann Patchett's dog—but for now, we just want to thank her deeply for bringing her ebullient touch to this book's Foreword.

Finally, to Dirk Walter, who helps us pull together our Smiling Dogs feature in each issue of the magazine, and Daniela Lopez, who wrangles the online smilers, our heartfelt thanks. And our special obeisance to Susan Tasaki, *Bark's* indefatigable, unflappable, keen-eyed senior editor.

# INDEX

Dudley & Cooper | Ollie | Lucy | Hobie, Dundee & Bodie | B-Bop | Rainy & Smoke

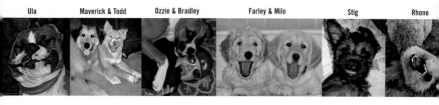

## ABOUT US

*The Bark* has been making dogs and their people smile since its launch twelve years ago as the leading voice of modern dog culture. It was the first magazine to focus on the bond between humans and canines. Since then, *Bark* has become essential reading for everybody who lives by its motto—*Dog Is My Co-Pilot*. Hailed as "the *New Yorker* of dog magazines," it has been honored with numerous awards for its distinctive design and distinguished writing. To learn more about the magazine and to see additional smiling dogs, visit us online at www.thebark.com.

*Bark* magazine was co-founded by Claudia Kawczynska and Cameron Woo, and is published in Berkeley, California. The editors have published two literary anthologies, the best-selling *Dog Is My Co-Pilot* and a humor collection, *Howl.* They live with their dogs, Lola, Lenny, and smilers-in-training, Holly and Kit.

*Bark* would love to see your smiling dogs. Please send your photos to us at smiling@thebark.com.

## FOREWORD

Ann Patchett has spent the last 14 years attending to the needs of her dog, Rose. In her few free moments she has managed to write several books, including *Bel Canto, Truth & Beauty, Run,* and *What Now?*

Bella

31901050473356